Love Is Deeper Than Distance

Poems of love, death, a little sex, ALS, dementia,
and the widow's life thereafter

by Peg Edera

Fernwood
PRESS

Love Is Deeper Than Distance

ISBN 978-1-59498-052-7

To my best teachers—Fred, Mia, and Annalee

Contents

Introduction

In 2010, my husband, Fred, was diagnosed with frontal temporal lobe dementia. Nine months later he was diagnosed with ALS. He was 65. With an enormous amount of loving care from friends and family, our daughter and I managed to care for him at home until his death, shortly after he turned sixty-seven.

The world of illness and dying is demanding and complex. I often was overrun by the stuff of caretaking, the extreme learning curve, the need for the very leaky boat of our hearth and home to stay afloat, the acute loneliness of missing him before he was gone, worry for our daughter, and grieving in all its dimensions and untimeliness.

A few of these poems were written before his diagnoses, many written during those eighteen months, and some written after his death as our lives continued without him. Writing helped me find the tender truth, the unlikely humor, the faithful awareness of the deep-hearted love that we shared with each other, our daughter and this unpredictable world, and what else may be.

Acknowledgments

I want to acknowledge all of my teachers. I am so grateful for all I have learned from you and all I continue to learn. I am so fortunate in your care.

My daughter Mia whose bright spirit embodies the best of us. You teach me every day how to be a loving woman and mother.

Fred and Annalee, who taught me how death doesn't end love or relationships; it just isn't how we planned it.

Terry, friend, sister, aunt—who taught me that huge and wonderful things can begin in unlikely ways.

Sue, who teaches me how to live wholeheartedly and is my North Star, guiding me home through the dark.

My sister Kathy, who taught me that a voice on the other end of the phone can change everything.

David, who taught me about the wonder and wisdom of waiting patiently for new beginnings.

My Quaker teachers: Mike Huber, Mark Pratt-Russum and West Hills Friends. Mike, who called me home to the still, quiet place I hadn't been able to find. Mark, who teaches us beautiful lessons about being Quaker in a changing world. West Hills Friends for teaching me about the faithfulness of community and for giving me the gift of a Care Committee. You are all in these pages.

My writing teachers: the Wednesday morning writing group, Esther, Sarah, and Deborah; Birch and Tina, and John Fox, Kim Stafford, and Luis Alberto Urrea. As you have comforted and coached, cajoled and pushed me, your words have formed and enlivened me. None of this without you.

Eric Muhr and Fernwood Press for teaching me one more lesson in manifestations of the impossible.

All the teachers I haven't named. If you think your name should be here, truly it should. If I listed you all, I would write endlessly. Instead, I just say thank you, thank you, thank you.

Less Than a Second

Less than a second
is the time it takes to fall in love.
  That summer night
  you walked out of the bright house
  on to the dark deck
  ready for the next day's wedding,
  already celebrating every damn thing
  anyone could think of,
  laughter floating out of your pores
  like fireflies.
  I can still hear the booming
  voice in my head
  Oh my God she never told me,
  and I walked out onto the lawn,
  looking back,
  the only fireflies were all around you,
  and the laughter called
  me back to the circle
  I never left again.

Less than a second
     is all it takes
     for the truth to be known,
     for the sadness to cover me
     as I admit you will never laugh
     with all your heart again,
     for me to see you sitting there gone,
     for me to remember
     who you really are.

It's a Miracle, I Tell You

The staccato rain on the roof
The sudden parting of clouds

The silent worship of morning
The kettle's steamy clicking on the stove

The stellar jay defending the nest
The gang of crows flying off

The 100 bones of feet
The climbing of mountains

The slenderness of throat
The fullness of hymns on Sunday

The meeting of you
The knowing of me

I tell you, it's a miracle

Proposal

I remember the night
you asked me to marry you—
pitch dark, tar dark,
a lightless night under pines,
in a tent on a spit of land,
more sound than light or solid ground.
Waves rolling stones and distant thuds of logs
meeting land,
we lie there, my head
on your shoulder.

I said
It's been six months—maybe

we should talk

about this relationship

sometime.

The dark is impenetrable, solid,
the surf rolls stones,
logs thud,
stones roll out,
I think you are asleep.
I shrug this off,
hoping that courage
returns with the light,
and then
into this deep black night
you softly say
Let's get married.
I laugh, astonished,
I can't see you.

Lilacs

Between the last customer
and morning light
in the parking lot of the Korean Gentlemen's Club,
he picks lilacs for me.
Standing high against a warehouse wall,
these always bloom early, and
he goes annually, covertly, in the still dark,
unsure of welcome by the
Korean Gentlemen.
He fills the car.

I imagine that damp, spring-scented ride home,
his fantasy of being busted for predawn lilac theft,
the evidence transferred to the squad car,
covering him and his lovely guilt
entirely, the police becoming drunk on the
heady enclosed amore of fragrance
and driving him home instead,
helping us get out all our vases,
filling them while the coffee brews.

What I Don't Want to Hear

My health insurance got cancelled last week.
This
I do not want to hear.
I do not care that I can
reinstate it today.
I do not care that I emerge
five days later, insured
and unscathed.
I am not grateful for the miracle
of good health which
is not a small miracle.
I do not want to hear
that I have to do it all
now alone.
My back-up man is gone—
the one who's had my back,
the one who picked up
the pieces of my busy-ness,
the one who made sure there was milk
for cereal because
he loved his morning latte,
so I didn't worry about milk.
He still loves his morning latte
but forgets milk.

I don't want to hear
that we will evolve
into a muddy, moldy ruin
sooner than we must
if I do not
pay attention.
Pay attention now
to all the things
all the time.
I do not want to let the metaphors
slip away when they soak up
too much of my brain,
my ability to focus
on the bills,
the milk, the tires,
the phone, the sheets,
the overflowing gutters.

MRI

No stopping today.
No wandering through the tall, lean trees,
the cells of my longest secrets.
This is not the day for my secrets.
This is the day for his secrets,
his rubbled landscape,
his crumbled high ground
to be finally seen.
This is the time for the next
unsettling of the unsettling,
for the revealing of his
splinter-timbered mind
that is not him but hides him
now beneath debris I can't move,
I just stand in, forlorn,
saying, that brick was once your
humor, this mortar your curiosity,
the broken window enthusiasm.
I am your last witness.

Crossing the Bridge

For Terry

I want to write a poem
as light and bright as we were
walking across the long wooden bridge
over the tidal river dividing the point
from the miles of white sandy beach and cold Atlantic.
I always stretched over the splintered gray railing,
peering at the horseshoe crabs
doing their strange dance across the sand bar.
The ungainly, prehistoric brown helmet shells
set me shuddering even in
the dancing heat of midday.
We were swaying long limbs and blowing hair,
deep tans, short shorts,
sighs and laughter and smart enough to know
no one could give us advice
wise enough for us to hear.

Twelve years later I met your brother
at your wedding. Our babies
became cousins, our ability to listen improved,
our hips widened, and we whispered
to each other memories
we couldn't tell the kids.
The husbands respected us more each year,
and our impatience with their absences
ebbed and flowed.

Now, forty years later, in this week
after your daughter's wedding,
we drink our tea from our
never empty cups, watch
crows fledge and eagles cross this bay
between firs black against
the blue, sun-streaked Pacific.

As my husband fades away now,
your husband is our constant light,
and we know we are not smart enough anymore.
We sit here side by side,
and tears slide silently down my face so often
I think I must have saved them for you,
for this quiet time
we witness together what's been
and this long empty time
stretching into what is
for how long we don't know.

Why Is the Question I Usually Leave Behind

Dinner last night
with people determined
to know us
even when your words
are shy and hiding
and your restlessness interrupts
like a sudden wind,
blowing hats off heads.
And so why returns.
Why go?
Why now?
Why this encounter
when there is so little of you
that they can find?
I thought they might be experts,
both being doctors,
but their expertise
is not for us.
I thought then there would be
some golden-threaded connection
discovered over dessert
that made it clear,
a sudden waking of what we share.

Perhaps we are a mirror they might need,
a patient image of how to be
when there's not much left to do.
Maybe we are resources for them
even though we feel our own
drying up like brittle grass
in September fields.
Maybe we are stories
for their quiet mornings
just before day rise
when they see each other in faint light
and speak of us,
remembering to whisper
thank you.

I Could Ask for One More Trip

I could ask for one more trip
to see the Cézannes at the d'Orsay.
I could ask for your humor
creating ripples of laughter
through the party,
a good-hearted stone thrown
in the pool of our friends.
I could ask for your endless exclamations of the best—
the best chocolate,
the best pasta,
the best walk,
the best concert,
the best of everything
meeting you on the lips, the eye, the ear,
the heart.
I could ask that we rock our grandchildren together.
So I ask for you.
I just ask for you.
I just ask for you that these days have sweetness
and as things dim, you are not afraid.

I ask for you that no matter how many years are left,
no matter how you are,
you feel, if nothing else,
the ground of love
solid beneath your feet by day
and the soft wrapping of love around
you in this dark.

Safe Home

I bring it to you
the safe home of me
the tea and toast and poems
like honey
I wish it for you
in starlight and sing it for you
in day rise it rests
on the fine dust of stillness
I whisper safe home
and hear your echo back
the one you secret deep away
in case you can offer it
and it can be received
I receive from far away
safe home
and kiss your forehead
that beautiful shining space of you
that opens like a shell
worn by the sand and sea of your constancy

Slowly I'll Take the Rest of My Life

Slowly I'll take the rest of my life
to love you well.
On the days I am impatient,
I will remember the waiting
birds on nests.
When I am sad,
I will sit down.
To love you well takes all
of my time.
The past, present like a limb,
always part of me.
The present, the whole of me at it
like skin, and the future
whistling away,
the pan pipes of maybe.
Slowly I learn this:
nothing more is needed,
keep learning,
love you well,
then say farewell.

The Transmissions of Open Heartedness

This is all I have left to do for you.
Yes, I will keep the house clean,
and I promise I will feed you when you can't.
I will show you pictures, most of them filled
with candle light, full plates,
old friends and family
and glasses of wine around the table
we have kept at center.
Some of them will be with children,
ours and the strays
we have tended along the way
as though they were ours.
We will walk when you can,
and I will point out flowers, dogs,
and cheerful neighbors. Some will bring their dogs
to you and leave flowers on the front steps.

And I will keep my heart open.
I will do this because,
in the end,
it's all I can do.
Greet you each day with
this heart of mine radiating
my belief in goodness.
Yours and mine.
This steady wild life we've lived together.
The world's slow turning
proving my point when
I let gravity have its way.

I Am More Alive Now

I am more alive now
standing beside you
in your numbered days.
My hair is brighter,
my eyes darker,
I stand straighter and laugh louder,
and it is only contrast,
the magic effect of not dying now.

Your eyes, always a bit unfocused
from an old accident,
are now focused on me
as though I am the only sure
and unmovable constant
in the swirl of light and color
we call house and kettle,
candle, phone and fork.

I can almost see your compensations
now like soldiers you employ,
the ranks dwindled
to just the stalwart survivors
of habit and appetite,
impulse and rhythm.
They are your heroes now
and mine
until they rest at last.

Assignment

When someone grips your shoulder
and shakes you awake
and you are alone in the dark room,
you could turn over,
burrowing into soft blankets,
and just before slipping back
into your own dark,
think dream.
Or you could wonder
who wants me awake
while others sleep?
You could ask if it's an angel,
impatient with all the distractions,
demanding you listen now.

Last night I listened,
and only lilting sadness came into me.
It was a quiet note or two,
then more, and the lyric was a lament,
a woe, a pity me, and it became
chains wrapping me to the bed,
the air tinged with iron—
I could no more move than die.

This morning I ache all over,
having done the hard work assigned.

Contours

Your mind is becoming a cloud,
edgeless, all the sharpness fading,
obscured by formless matter
sensed but nothing we can handle.
It is subtle thievery every day,
this disappearing.

Your day is a litany now
of what has been and is.
What will be, we avoid in the light hours.
The dark hours bring it in,
the interference of walkers, tubes, braces,
the questions of after that,
the fear of pain,
my fear of not knowing your fear.

A litany is only a list,
but a good litany is a gateway—
every name a truth,
a beauty, a memory,
a promise to you of remembering.

Now while the contours blur and dissolve,
and definitions disappear,
hold my hand.
I'll stroke your knuckles,
the knob of your wrist.
I'll run my finger around
the shell of your nails,
and right in the middle of your palm,
I'll fill the hollow with my thumb.

Messages

I can feel them,
the ones who have gone on,

gone on before those of us
still flexing the long bones

of our fragile feet on the soft earth.
They feel like whispers and

stray ends of webs and
dangling threads,

sometimes a little prickly,
a small thorn easily brushed away

or the tiny breeze on a humid day
lifting the hairs on the back of my neck.

I see them in the light of leaves
shifting in the wind I can't feel.

When I am still enough
and scrounge enough courage

up from the heart
that does not always want to hear

the messages that others don't,
I'll ask then why they're back.

Today I can imagine their answers,
and without the risk of disrespect,

change what I don't want to know just yet.
Today they say we're here to help.

Your one man is coming our way.
While he feels he's hollowing,

maybe we can fill him in
with what lies ahead.

If he can't hear us, you can,
and then you whisper our whispers to him.

Be our translator.
He'll hear you, his best voice,

the one he wants to hear last,
joined with Mia's voice

who just shouldn't hear us yet.

I've Been Writing You Songs

I've been writing you songs
this whole long year.
That's why I'm taking singing lessons—
to sing
to you.
I'll wait though
until you can only hear
the love
and pass on
with it in your ear.

The rest of the songs
I have for you
are unnumbered,
and I'll write them
even when you can't hear them,
even when I sing only to air.

I think I'll write you songs forever.
Even though I might
write a few for other fellows,
there will always be a line
that's just for you.

And when I sing,
I'll sing the sad parts loud.

I Promise You

When you go, I will send
a part of me with you.
Don't worry, it will be
the part that belongs with you,
not a part that I need
for carrying on.

When I go, I will carry
you like a magic seed
that I can sprout in the
night again and again—
each bloom will bear a
picture of you, and I will
kiss it as morning comes.

When I go, I will go
quietly. You will hardly
notice the door closing.
It will be a slipping
away like air stilling
after a faint breeze, and
you will smell
lilies of the valley and smile.

I will tell you,
while you can still hear,
a fairy tale, and you'll remember
always that together we saved
villages from wild beasts
and turned foul water
into clear tumults of waterfalls
and that we knew how to
cry for the children.

I will write you poems that
you'll find in your shoes
and under the sheets,
stuck on your belt buckle
and between the pages of cookbooks.
You will know
you are loved between time,
this life, the last, the next.

Meditation

Yesterday I was clasped hands—
your hard worn, chipped nail hand
in my well veined, heavy knuckled hand.
The wrapping of our years together,
the hollow space inside the clasping,
the green room
we grew our daughter in.

Today I am open handed—
the cup of them a drinking place,
the valley of them
a place for butterflies to land and leave,
a departure here
and a safe return.

Today I am still,
the container inside unshakable,
the container outside moving.
I am a secret now—
what you see and what is,
so different.
I am waiting time.
I am the still point
inside the twinkling change.

The Yankee Girl Builds One More Woodpile

How do I know I am ready for winter?
Dry split hard wood, stacked close to the house.
Splinters in the fleshy mound below my thumb.
Broken fingernails.
Bark tangled in my hair.
The muscles between neck and shoulder blade become a plank.
Bare feet in the morning are unpleasant,
and the woodpile is as high as my chin and
three times as long.

What makes a wood pile more than a woodpile?
A sick husband.

The Promise I Can Keep

Twenty-three years ago our daughter,
our first-born, died,
and now you are waning.
The grip of ALS and dementia grows like
talons sinking slowly deeper,
and this marking, this anniversary
of all our annual remembrances—
    the day alone together,
    looking at photographs,
    pretending they are not fading,
    telling the memories that float up like old leaves,
    suddenly released and catching light,
    from the bottom of a deep lake,
    the trip to the grave site
    where we clean the stone
    and whisper our messages,
    leaving flowers and letters,
    kisses placed on the cold gray granite—
this year your tears were promises
that I made for you.

You were so sad

that you would not see her again

as though each anniversary was a visit,

a day you held her against your shoulder again,

your cheek gentle by hers,

and as you see your end,

you cannot see your reuniting.

So I promised you today, and I promise

this tomorrow

    what happens next is not empty.

If it was

we would not have held her

for twenty-three years.

I promise you.

I promise you.

Writing Poetry, I Burned the Squash:
A Lesson in What Is Real

The unexpected lowing of a train
has echoed all day.
I called my neighbor to check
if my ears had trumped up this
mechanical howl.
She said,
Yes, that's the case. I haven't heard a thing.
There it is I said.
Nothing she said.
Maybe it's the gnome you saw squatting on the sidewalk.
Give me a break, I said, *he stood up and*
we both saw him—just a short man all dressed in red.
This is a train. Not coyotes. Really.
She hung up.
I wondered
if it is just this city
telling me a long train
is leaving the station.
My husband says no when he means yes sometimes
and sometimes says yes for no,
and sometimes he says what he means,
but I'm never sure now.
Maybe it is just the slow wail
of another car in his train uncoupling.

March

The trudge of your illness
is a silent pilgrimage

to an unholy place.
Is that sacrilege?

The destination, I know,
is the Temple of What Is Next.

The trudge of it all
is the gray, quiet column

of weary, shocked soldiers,
and it is inside you,

relentless in its slow winding
that is your bird-less, clouded landscape.

And there is no Holy anything
there.

The Holy lens is broken
in this morning's light.

It is only the trudge,
tired foot before sore one,

the path unclear,
the work to do still undone,

all your companions weary, too.

This Week

Your frail vocabulary
divided in half this week.
I understand being alone is too lonely.

Now that you are my constant companion,
I scramble to do
what is to be done
in the time to do it in.
Unless you are asleep
you are my too-tight shirt,
the glove that binds,
the scarf around my neck,
caught in the door.

Last night you said
I can't wait ...
I can't wait ...
I can't wait to die.
Every day brings a new sadness.

Today the beach was silver,
the water blue and gold.
Walking the flat, windless, sun-covered sand,
we could become silver-skinned.
When you walked ahead,
I thought
keep on,
become silver,
don't look back,
and if you do
I'll be here watching
until you are the faintest shadow,
until I see you
even though you are gone.

Making Dinner

Standing at the cutting board
singed with a black, half circle,
the big knife I love to cut onions with
balanced in my right hand,
I think suddenly of what else
the blade could do
and when and where I'd find myself
if I were to wield it differently.
It is your silent absence, the disappearing snap of your neurons,
the faint emptying tremble of your hand,
the unblinking, unspoken question in your eyes,
it is my quiet resignation to do right by you
and this time of dull leaden light
of early evening in Oregon,
the state of rain shadow
and vitamin deficiencies and perseverance.
It is the future like a too-thin blanket
stretching not far enough
for the warm dreams
to hang on until morning,
that set me to the indulgence
of what else I would cut
if I could.

The evening drill of chop and stir
is no longer the pleasant end,
the marker of what's been,
and meditation on what's next,
the salting and baking the mother does,
or what the lover prepares.
It is now the long breath,
the steeling time, the mustering of
the bright face.
The hours left before we fade in sleep
are slowly sadder every night.
Tonight I'd cut minutes.

Maybe It's a Mercy

I want to write about divorce.
It's such a harsh word,
and I've done it before.
I won't really do it now,
at least not in the way
legal is real.
But I am uncoupling us,
and maybe it's a mercy,
letting you go so you can go,
letting you go so I can
begin the salvage job
even though you're here yet
for an unknown stretch of time,
just your husk,
your shell
and every now and then a glimmer
breaking through enough
so that I bow down in the tiny ray
giving thanks
for all the time
I knew the full beam of you.

Merry Christmas, Baby

10:00 Christmas night, washing dishes,
new headphones plugged into the iPod,
you started to sing
like Tom Waits singing James Brown,
hoarse, gravelly,
a spoon in one hand, a glass in the other,
your pants sagging down low from lost weight
like a rapper without intent.
At first you didn't know we heard you,
or maybe you didn't know you were singing.
Then you saw us, a grin spread across
your stony face,
the song changed and Delbert McClinton was singing
Midnight Communion,
and you sang every word.
Streaming out your mouth,
more words than we'd heard in three days.

What's Coming

Monday
The next clinic,
4 hours of specialists,
this one includes Hospice.

Wednesday
Our daughter
moves home from university.
Sophomore year unfinished.
Courage, her biggest school.

Feeding you.
Washing you.
Interpreting for you.

Panic.

Decisions.

Crying.
Dying.
Surviving.
Living.

The Wooing

An hour before we entered
the year you will probably die,
we turned to The Book of Changes.
The hexagram cast was titled
The Wooing.
Is this the last wisdom of this hard year,
or is it the new wisdom to carry forward?

As last wisdom I remember the ways
you have wooed me for 26 years.
This is a better exercise
than sorting the recent memories of
your ever increasing absence,
your sadness,
and resolve to ignore
what couldn't be denied.

As new wisdom, it calls me to remember my job—
which is to love you—
despite the rising rubble of taxes
and refinancing, Social Security and insurance,
all the things
that need forms filled out perfectly.

If I remember to love you,

if I remember that that is the job

of seeing you through and helping you over,

I see what woo really means now.

I get to woo you,

court you,

entice you

to the brink,

the end of days,

to the good goodbye.

Now That You Are Home

Now that you are home,
there is a small peaceful lake inside me,
just below my diaphragm,
in the middle of the plumb line,
the balance point balanced and warm.

I thought your return home to help Dad die
would be sadness,
pale cheeks and bloodshot eyes,
bruised chapped lips
and gray clothes.
I thought it would be rage,
a slamming door and accusations,
broken glass,
the teapot boiled dry.
I thought it could be a void,
an empty room,
your shadow on the bed
stifling gasps
only a Mother hears
in the late nights that never end.

Instead we are two women watching.
The witnesses on his hillside, steady,
eyes open through the cold nights
and stormy days, unflinching,
steadfast,
borrowing the strength
of women through time,
standing by their men,
saying, *yes, you are leaving,*
and we are not.
We'll hold your last threads,
the faint wisps of your soul,
until the wind blows just enough.

Why I Don't Go out Much Anymore

If you could speak,
you might say
Abandon fixing me.
You might say
Thy will be done
and mean it through and through,
but you can't speak much more than
Yeah and the occasional surprise like
I visited with the community of saints last night.
And when I told you
the bath helper Amanda was coming
and I asked if that was OK,
Yeah, you said.
And then you looked me in the eye and said
I'm naked you know.
And the time you told our pastor
the song you wanted at your memorial service was
Why Don't We Do It in the Road.
The best was when you told Mia
Love is deeper than distance.

What I Miss Today

I'd like to hear you say
I love you
one more time in passing.
One of the casual utterances,
an afterthought as I walked by
because it happened to fall out of your mouth
just then.
That's what I miss today.
That little moment that happened
often enough that it was
part of the air, part of the dust,
part of the things I only partially heard,
moving from kitchen to bath,
from pan to sink to car to now.

My Part Is Witness

My part is witness and memory bearer.
I keep them in an old pottery jar,
the color of fresh earth washed with iron.
The meeting, the wedding, the babies, the aging parents,
the work, the babies, the trips,
they all fit inside.
Whenever one more rises, I lift the lid
and tuck it in where it is safe.

My part is witness and nursemaid.
I clean the dishes that seem to sprout
in our sink all day long.
I clean the sheets and toilets
and all the tools of comfort
I've never seen before.
I plump the pillows and
remind you to brush your teeth
and remember to crush your pills
thoroughly into the applesauce
and answer the doctor's questions
like I'm sitting for my
graduate exams.

My part is witness and hospitality staff.
I welcome the friends
and the food they bring.
I try to keep the flowers fresh
and the dust invisible.
When I need more help I remember
how much I like to help
and trust that someone else will, too.
I ask carefully
and say thank you
again and again.

My part is witness and widow-to-be.
I try to prepare,
keep the bills paid, the car repaired.
I try to pay my taxes.
I try to imagine how many tears
I will cry in public.
I try not to ask questions
I can't answer yet.
I keep a file of what could be next.

My part is witness and chief mourner.
I am to cry
and rip my clothing,
and I can't
because when you go
you will have lived so well.

Summer Without You

It is July 23, 2012,
and I haven't gone
to the farmers market yet.
Really, it is the best of the Pacific Northwest.
The berries in their voluptuous tumults collide
with black-eyed Susans and
red leaf lettuce big as weeds,
and lavender, lavender
contained and elegant,
purple spikes fragrant like sharp memories,
early fuchsias overflowing their boundaries,
just wild ballerinas beside
rotund radishes.

I haven't seen them yet
because this was your sure passion
every Saturday morning.
A quick stop at the ATM, and you surged
down the aisle, mission obsessed
from booth to stall
knowing the beans and corn and cukes,
the tomatoes and basil, onions
and those very best peaches
that were right there in that left corner
near the back.

They would tell you
these were the best this week,
and you'd buy a flat.
Every week.

In May our daughter went on
opening day for the summer season.
She came home crying.
You were at every beautiful cascade
of early lettuce, radicchio
and the uprising of fresh bitter tang
the dirt-bound root, arugula,
and clash of orange geranium against
blue lobelia and green fern
and worshipful turn of corner
sighing into the best
of this season
that to you always was too fleeting.

I could be sad.
I could write chapters about
how the market spoke to you.
I could say you canned peaches every year
because the golden jars preserved
were sunlight to you,
but now I know
they were preservations
of what you could still save
when we didn't really comprehend that you
couldn't comprehend
that peaches are just moments of summer
meant to live just the months they last
from tree
to pot
to can
to mouth.

Love Songs

The word we use is
dead
for your current state of being.
Inadequate and even silly
this assumption
of complete absence.
It's true I don't wake with you beside me now.
But sometimes I wake
to a waterfall of music
falling into my waking ears,
and there you are,
loving me still.

My eyes adored you
Like a million miles away from me
You couldn't see how I adored you
So close, so close and yet so far
Fools rush in where angels fear to tread
And so I come to you my love

Temperatures rising, I don't want to feel
I'm in the wrong place to be real
And I'm longing to love you
Just for a night

Family Ritual

In the Italian restaurant
where Italian language lessons
are piped into the bathrooms like opera
we convene in the last minutes
of happy hour
sliding into wicker chairs, speed-ordering
before prices change.
The traffic sucks, Mike's late,
parking impossible, Gary
parked one tire up on the curb.
Vida walked down,
roses in full bloom, and
the neighbors brought over strawberries.
Terry says the view in the new house
of Mt. Saint Helens
is beautiful.

My back is to an iron railing,
Fred and Gene are leaning against it.
I can feel them there,
the ones who went on before us,
just out of sight.
They knew they would find us here,
the wine a grassy gold
in fading light.

Crossing the Border

On your way from Canada
you sit nestled into
the new boy-man
on a full bus heading here,
to home, the one you grew in,
weed-rangy and sometimes
mad-dog crazy.
The bus lumbers through dark into gray morning,
the Pacific Northwest change of blue-less light,
and right now you are at the air-tense border
as the mental checklist
for pipes and joints and pills
rolls through the collective conscience.
You nestle in and tell him
not to worry about me,
the mother, the only parent now,
facing this vetting,
each of us for the first time,
without the father
to crack the stupid joke,
make the awkward gesture,
cut the tension of making good impressions,
of weighing the whole looming future—

and to start the laughter
that is as much glue here
as the full table, the candles,
the wine and the crackling firelight.
You say
Don't worry,
underneath it all she is kind.
She loves me.

I'd Like a Different Job

I understand that archeology
is slow and painstaking.
You crouch in old dust
with little tools, picks and brushes,
gently blowing away
everything old that is formless.
Very carefully you preserve
every bit and shard,
cataloging every scrap
by the inch of depth
in the selected dirt.

Now that you are gone,
I am the archeologist of our lives.
I would like to be the backhoe operator,
getting it done by the bucketful
so that the ground we stood on so long
looks new, ready to plant
regardless of the buried bits below.

I understand, though, that I am
to slowly measure and weigh,
holding to the light the old
as though it's new
and worth more than its clay
because it is really
a broken piece of a bigger story.

One Wish

Today's choice would be
that we all sit together
for one more dinner of bouillabaisse—
the red saffron broth
filled with fine mysteries of sea life
so different
from our gravity-bound earth life.
We can only give thanks
that they swam to net to mouth
in moon and candlelight.

Yesterday's choice would be
for my girl
so that as I left
she would always know
her mother's love
like a cashmere shawl around her shoulders
and wear it like a warrior's shield
and use it for the magic
it will ever be.

Tomorrow's wish
would be that
all the love-filled wishes
come true.

A New Hard Place—A History of the Widow's Bed to Date

At first the bed without you
was a wide oasis.
The distance between us those last months
grew drier than the Sahara.
As you left us before your body left,
the only way I knew
to save my heart from more cracking
was to sleep on the sofa,
but I couldn't leave you alone
in the night.

At first the bed without you
was the place I could still
feel you with me
even though the nights before you died
were the longest loneliness.
I would lie on the soft, clean sheets,
breathe in the soft scent of roses,
and turn, putting my head
on your ephemeral shoulder.
Being able to really rest with you
after all these months,
I wouldn't move for hours.

At first the bed was more a cradle.
Here I was all alone.
The days were filled with forms
and phone calls.
At night the crowded business of death
could settle around me.
I could cover myself with the soft blanket
embroidered with *done for now*.
It was a refuge of solitude,
and my first prayer was
thank you, bed.

After awhile the bed
became the place I stayed too long.
It was a cave in winter
that slowly became
a hiding place.

After awhile I would startle
awake at 3 am.
My first thought was
you had come to visit.
My second thought, the memory
that no one else had been here
but me
for a long time.

Last night the pillows were hard and lumpy.
The soft sheets were hot and musty.

All I wanted was a memory I don't have.
All I wanted was the sound of your voice saying
You were always my best dream come true.
I wanted that one letter explaining
how I had changed your life into something
more beautiful than butterflies.

And now in the cold morning
I doubt I was ever more than
a decent cook, a lot of fun,
a pretty good bed mate,
the mother of your child.
If I asked our friends they would testify
willingly
that we had good
and beautiful years.

But I'm asking you.
Show me some irrefutable sign.
Lilacs falling through the clouds.
Love songs sung by birds.

So Long

More than 1,000 days
since I saw you last,
our daughter flew to Haiti.
If you were here, we'd argue,
our anxieties unsyncopated.
Yours rising, as I am noticing
the sun on wet ferns.
My annoyance with your worry
growing like yeasted dough in a warm oven.
Then you would make espresso
as I *what if'd*
for the 100th time before breakfast,
the hiss of hot steam drowning out
my fretful drone.
If you were here I would
roll in the night,
fitting leg to knee, hip to hip,
my head could find
the hollow of your shoulder and chest
and you wouldn't wake
and I would rest
thinking those stars
I can see through the lace curtain,
those stars shine on her, too.

Home for the Holidays

I could feel you, daughter,
coming home in the late night.
I opened the door so light would spill out
onto the granite stones you'd walk down.
I waited
feeling for the displaced air
of the car turning the corner,
feeling for the sound of rain pattering through the trees
to thrum with the under rhythm of the car.
I stepped out,
bare feet on the wet stones,
my breath faintly curling white into the darkness.
The rain fell on my hair,
glistening little drops in the light.
The rain fell on my bare feet,
startling me just enough
to not hear the first sounds until you turned the corner.
And I thought:
This waiting was exquisite.

Expectations

By now I would have met
at least one man who
warmed my blood and tasted of cloves.
By now I would have settled
my routines of days end
and evenings arrival.
I would have stopped
thinking of you so often
even though half of my life
was spent with you.
I would have a different access
to puns and witty metaphors.
Instead I have a few
nice fellows I easily keep
off my shore like sail boats
tacking back and forth across my harbor.
Instead I have a restless worry
as day shortens that this night
will be too long,
that sleep will be a distant cousin
instead of a sister holding my hand.

I have a marching band of memories
filled with you
distracting, entertaining and
playing songs
I have heard too often.
I have a spark of humor
that lights up the room
but not the house.

Five Months In

When I speak of him
their sweet ears
perk up delicately
like a sleeping cat—
not an over-reaction,
just a quick response
to something new in the room.
They raise their eyebrows
when I speak of him.
They even question my
reservations about him.
They doubt my doubts.
I think it is just desire—
their desires
for one more love story
to enter our wintry years.
It is their well wishing
that I may have
one more boon companion—
the fluttering hope,
if it happens for her
it might for me.

I don't even know
if he can dance.

Nothing Is Ever Finished

When our first daughter died,
I understood she was still
with me.
I told our second daughter that
I carry her sister in my heart.

When you died
I remembered that
you were gone,
but we were not done.

As long as I am remembering you,
we are still something together.

Now it is
the physical memory
that wakes me at night.
The biggest piece missing
of each of you
is touch.

To Keep This House

To keep this house
        I pay the mortgage and taxes,
        I worry about the gutters,
        the peeling paint on the
        east side, the moss
        on the driveway, the great
        sequoia limbs falling
        in storms on my roof,
        the neighbor's roof.
To keep this house
        I escort the spiders and mice
        out the door,
        reminding them they like
        the greater space more
        than they think.
        I let the squirrels run
        and dig, the birds pull worms
        and sing, the frogs do their
        deep throated calling and
        the cat pretend she is a
        lion in the savanna.

To keep this house
      I sweep. I mop.
      Sometimes I vacuum.
      I wash the sheets, the curtains.
      I open the windows
      and let the wind blow through.
      I get the big windows washed
      by a fellow who likes light
      almost as much as I do.
To keep this house
      I wake early and sit facing
      the ring of big trees,
      following the fade of night
      into prayers like breath
      and sometimes beseeching.
      I welcome anyone
      who is feeling lost so they
      can remember who they are
      and that they are
      safer than they were
      before they got here.
      To keep this house,
      this house and I
      hear their prayers.

Last Night at Dinner

You said, "Let's make-out on the Promenade."
Your white hair and beard
framing your eyes twinkling
like some misbehaving star.
I should have lifted my shirt,
flashed you some skin,
met your boy with my girl,
letting the other diners faint
or catch you as you did.

Love Wants

Love wants a little tip of the hat,
the wink, the wry smile
that passing acknowledgment
that Love really is the fuel,
that Love really is all around.
Love loves to be Coyote,
shifting from roses to ashes
in the blink of an eye.
Love gets merry,
puts on tap shoes and leaps on the table
when we remember
we are holding on too tightly
and asking Love to look
like just one thing.
Love gets proud when we know
what isn't Love and walk away.
Then Love wants us to pop a cigar in our mouths,
uncork the champagne.

Love loves a pun and
the double entendre.
Love loves the big meal
eaten outside under the full moon.
Love loves to show up unexpected.
Love is always holding our hands
at the bedside of the dying.
Every now and then Love wants us
to say thank you.

Honest Any Way—on the 29th Anniversary of My Daughter's Death

I want to speak about my woe.
When you ask, "How are you?"
I want to wail
if I have one quivering
right below the surface.
I want to say
I don't want to tell you.
I want you to sit down,
looking at me from behind your eyes
beckoning me to say
the only thing I really have to say.
I want you to touch my hand.
If you don't,
I want to forgive you.
I don't want to speak this
because my unfathomable grief
is more unfathomable than yours.
I don't want to do this
because I cannot contain it
or need your sympathy.
I want to speak about my woe
because on this day
it is the only honest answer
and
we should simply live there.

Four Christmases Without You

The carols were boisterous, sung around an old piano festooned
with ornaments, trinkets, cards from this year and years past.
We even videoed us all singing Happy Birthday to Pamela's mother—
a breathy, jazzy version sung to the tune of "The Girl from Ipanema."
You weren't there, but we all remembered you quietly
in the random pun, the witty anecdote, the odd fact
stored for years suddenly slipping out, surprising us
like a seal flipping through the door.
There was dinner with the stepfather and his daft wife,
my sister and her husband and Mia,
the shining star on our Christmas tree.
The food was the Christmas fish—salmon, of course,
peas and mushrooms, wild rice, salad—so easy and good.
A statement to abundance and moderation.
The last such statement until Boxing Day.
And then the Blessed Day itself.
No talk of Jesus except by email from my friends
still trying to sort out how a Holy Day
honoring an ancient man born of a virgin and then
rising from the dead—
how that was absconded by Macy's
and Target and Home Depot and Costco.
But here the day tipped its large hat
to the consumer church and then
all the neighbors began to visit us.

They loved you
and found our pain these last years
to look like a wound bleeding again and again.
And they came yesterday and didn't find us bleeding.
Together we just loved you,
wherever we think you are,
and we carried on and on
right along with you
even though you're gone.

Too Old

The night the foot massage,
familiar, friendly, a safe sensuality,
left me sleepless
was the night your soft hand
slipped casually under the edge
of my black jeans, up my ankle.
My eyes widened, and I swallowed
that intake of breath
that could have told us what could be.
That was the beginning of deciding
the cracked asphalt track
we had made together
could become the Silk Road.
Even though I was sleepless
I saw our track still as leading
to the same market,
the same four-pillared time we knew.
I insisted on it
until you reached the other ankle
and I thought
I am too old to say no.

Rx—Splitting the Order

In our early days
we met in restaurants
and shared our food with each other.
A small generosity, a welcoming,
a tiny intimacy in a public place.
Soon we grew confident enough
to order our meal and share it.
It was a good economy.
We were finding our togetherness
thorough the culinary world.
Now that we have progressed
all the way to the sharing of the bed,
I cook for you.
I fill earth-colored ceramic bowls
with bright vegetables
and lay the pink salmon
on the green plate with lemons.
Sometimes you do not like what I cook.
I feel bad but accept
that I do not yet know all your ways.

In our days to come,
let's remember to go out into the wider world
and find the café that will tolerate
our sharing.
We can find the meal we want to split,
look across the little table,
wondering again
what's next.

On the Third Anniversary of Meeting

In the morning I start with my toes
buried far away under the covers.
I wiggle them and say silently
Hello toes, and move on up
Hello feet, heels, ankles—
you get the picture.
By the time I get to my heart
I have thought of you at least once.

       Yesterday the persimmon hung
like lanterns on the edge of the koi pond
in the garden where we first met.
We perambulated slow circuits
past the waterfall and the thorny branches
of the dragon fruit bush, the late blooming azaleas
and the showy bank of chrysanthemums.
In the tea house we recalled
our first meeting, where we sat,
how our conversation began.

Then I said
If we ever decide to get married
you have to ask me
on a barge with silk cushions
in the middle of the river
under the full moon with a violinist playing
and koi shining in the water around us.
And you said,
Yes, but with a string quartet
and when I ask
the koi will jump out of the water
arching over us.

I Really Want to Be Your Valentine Well

Yesterday I read your poem
between letting the cat out
and pouring tea.
There was a line in there
I really liked,
and this morning I don't remember it.
Today I make a vow—
If you send me one more precious poem
written in the early morning
with your hair still wild from sleep,
your flannel pajamas still warm from the bed,
I will read it as though
I have waited all my life
for these exact words.
I may even call you
saying *read it to me*
and I will sink into your voice,
the warm pool of it,
submerging so
my hair floats like seaweed
in what you offer me
so readily,
only coming up for air
so I can submerge again
thankful.

Last Day of April

Yesterday I was asked
how I soften my heart
as though this was the desired state.
I agree with the premise
because my heart is rough and dry with scars
and does not feel as useful
as it did in other decades.
Let's assume I have a decade left,
maybe two if my cranky body
lingers longer than advised.
This soft-hearted premise
I welcome still,
more interested in the possibilities of joy
than frightened by the surety of grief.
Today I soften it with words like prayer:
Soften heart.
It's OK.
I'll be right here with you
through it all.

Fifth Christmas Without You

Our daughter did not
cry in the night this Christmas.
I didn't see her across the dinner table
crumble like a sandcastle pushed by waves.
How I miss you now is not the same.
I no longer have a gaping hole or
a sense of something gone like an arm.
How I miss you now is like a song in my head
that I can't quite hear and want to.
How I miss you now is like a cold spot
in the room that never quite gets warm.
It is like the sadness of a tree holding one last leaf,
like the field that is frozen grass
bent over until spring.
How I miss you is like pretty gloves that are too tight
and make my fingers colder.
It is like a chill, a swallow of almost sour milk,
like a meal without salt
and ball that doesn't bounce.
This year I didn't wish
that I had set a place at the table for you,
the reminder of your presence and our loss.
This year no gifts from you
made sense.

The new year ahead looks like a storm
that may never pass,
and I worry, again, about our daughter
and how to be her mother without her father.
Last night I reminded myself
to have faith in her
and the parts of her
that are you
and that are me.

Heartbreak

This is what you have to learn—
heartbreak is infinite.
Eventually you can tuck it in a small corner
you can live with,
even if he broke your arm in three places and you hate him,
even if she drank mezcal and wrecked your car on your birthday,
even if he guessed on the night you met
the name you picked at twelve for your first-born child
and you never saw him again,
even if he lived long and well and his death was overdue.
Any way you slice love
the leftover crumbs are heart break.
You can disagree and stop here,
avoid this pointing at one of the real things nobody wants to see
or you can remember
the origami-ed scrap of love
folded so tiny you have ignored it
like a speck of dust on your glasses.
It is there, I swear.
Sometimes the scraps fall out on the table
like an old valentine falls out of the book
your love gave you that first year.
You thought you had lost it
but no
it's been there all along,
each word a world shared.

This World Is a Museum of Love

Look around.
Every effort has love behind it or under it, beside it or in it.
The curiosity to pick up the one dark green stone,
that effort of curiosity is fueled by love,
the love of cool weight or sun-warmed weight, the love
of time and hardened earth, the love of the common thing.

The irises blooming their extravagant flouncy skirts
were planted intentionally.
That nesting in dirt a hope of love next year
spurred by the memory of love
in some other garden.

The fish caught in the late afternoon
under the changing, dipping sun
accompanied by flies and frogs,
the love of fish, the love of fresh, the love of skill,
the love of sharing and tasting,
the love of river and alone.

The clean sheets still smelling
of the line-dried wind, stretched across
the bed piled with shaken blankets,
reformed pillows,
the love of clean, the love of fresh (again),
of sleeping bodies waking in the dark,
the love of laundry and washing machines.

The dinner table itself a place of love.
The tablecloth and candlesticks
the love of time together, the crystal salt shaker
the love of the formal grandmother,
flowers the love of color and scent, dew and dirt,
food the love of change,
from raw to cooked to lips to sated,
the love of recipes shared, recipes perfected,
recipes forgiving.
The food the love of staying alive.
The dinner party the love of
these people.
Our love of words and smiles,
complex and confusing,
the too-loud laugh, the off-color joke,
the love of the ones who are missing,
the love of the ones yet to join us,
the love of love.

CPSIA information can be obtained
at www.ICGtesting.com
Printed in the USA
FSHW011817040219
55468FS